I0170985

Arahant Koṇḍañña

the

First Bhikkhu

මහාමේඝ
MAHAMEGHA

A Mahamegha Publication

Arahant Koṇḍañña the First Bhikkhu

Prajapati Jayawardena

ISBN : 978-955-687-168-5

Printed: Esala Full Moon Poyaday - 2562 B.E. (July. 2018)

Computer Typesetting by
Mahamevnawa Buddhist Monastery
Waduwawa, Yatigaloluwa, Polgahawela, Sri Lanka.
Telephone: +94 37 2244 602
www.mahamevnawabm.org

Published by
Mahamegha Publishers
Waduwawa, Yatigaloluwa, Polgahawela, Sri Lanka.
Telephone: +94 37 2053300 | +94 76 8255703
mahameghapublishers@gmail.com

For those who seek more in life ...

Contents

Acknowledgments

I would like to sincerely thank everyone who encouraged and supported me to make this book a reality. First and foremost, the Most Venerable Kiribathgoda Gnānānanda Thera, my mentor, my teacher, for his encouraging words and also all the other venerable monks of Mahamevnawa Buddhist Monastery for their advice, guidance, and encouragement, without whose support this story would never have reached publication. Also, Mrs. Tracy Mawson for proofreading. I must thank Mr. Yourin for the cover artwork, and also Mahamegha publishers. Last but not least, my husband, Mr. Dilupa Jayawardena for all the encouragement and support.

Introduction

This book narrates the story of Arahant Koṇḍañña, the first Bhikkhu in Gautama Buddha's Dispensation. When Koṇḍañña realized the Four Noble Truths by listening to the first sermon of the Lord Buddha 2607 years ago, the noble Saṅgha was born into this world.

In compiling this story, I referenced the great discourses Mahā Sīhanāda sutta and Ariya Pariyesena sutta of the Majjhima Nikāya.

The disciples of Lord Buddha are of four types: Bhikkhu–the monks, Bhikkhunī–the nuns, Upāsaka–laymen, and Upāsikā-laywomen. The term Saṅgha is used to address the disciples who have left lay life and ordained as renunciates. The males who go forth are thus called the Bhikkhu Saṅgha, and the females are called the Bhikkhunī Saṅgha; and together they are called Mahā Saṅgha The word Mahā is used for respect. Their purpose in life and the benefit they bring to others are described by the Lord Buddha, succinctly, in the well-known Pāli stanza:

Supatipanno bhagavato sāvakasaṅgho. Ujupatipanno bhagavato sāvakasaṅgho. Ñāyapatipanno bhagavato sāvakasaṅgho. Sāmīcipatipanno bhagavato sāvakasaṅgho. Yadidaṃ cattāri purisayugāni aṭṭha purisapuggalā esa bhagavato sāvakasaṅgho. Āhuneyyo, pāhuneyyo, dakkhineyyo, añjalikaranīyo, anuttaraṃ puññakkhettaṃ lokassā'ti"

Bhagavato sāvakasaṅgho – the Saṅgha of the Lord Buddha

Supatipanno – strives to eradicate greed, hatred, and delusion

Ujupatipanno – follows the Noble Eightfold Path which leads straight to Nirvāna

Ñāyapatipanno – strives to realize the Four Noble Truths

Sāmīcipatipanno – teaches the noble Dhamma

Yadidaṃ cattāri purisayugāni aṭṭha purisapuggalā – there are four pairs of disciples and eight when taken individually based on the disciple's stage of enlightenment

Āhuneyyo – they are worthy of offerings

Pāhuneyyo – they are worthy of hospitality

Dakkhineyyo – they are worthy of gifts, mainly the four requisites: robes, food, shelter, and medicine

Añjalikaranīyo – they are worthy of reverential salutation

Anuttaraṃ puññakkhettaṃ lokassā'ti – they are the unsurpassed field of merit for the world.

1

The Naming Ceremony

The young Brahmin Koṇḍañña could not believe his eyes. His heart stood still for a moment, and the hair on his body stood up as he took another closer look at the newborn Prince, who was lying on his back with his mother Queen Mahāmāya gazing down upon him affectionately. After attending many naming ceremonies, and having seen countless newborn babies, the Brahmin Koṇḍañña had finally met he for whom he had been looking ever so long. Everything he longed to see in a newborn baby was right in front of him. The most beautiful baby he had ever seen and the baby who would one day be his teacher was right in front of him. After a few moments of silence, owing to the exuberant joy in his heart, the Brahmin Koṇḍañña regained his composure and took a firm step forward.

"My Lord King, your son has only one path ahead of him, not two. He will not become an Emperor. He will become a Buddha, an Enlightened One."

The entire hall fell silent.

It is said that a thousand years ago a great commotion stirred in the Brahma world regarding the future arising of a Buddha. The commotion having spread to the deva world, further spread to the human world. Compassionate devas revealed to humans the prophecy of a future Buddha, encouraging them to do acts of merits, since in a thousand years-time a Buddha would arise in the world out of compassion for devas and humans to free them from saṃsāra. The devas advised, 'if you were to accrue enough merit you would be fortunate to listen to His teachings and realize the Dhamma.' Seers of the Himalayas having heard of this, were eager to learn how to recognize a Buddha if they should meet one. With the help of the devas they were able to learn of the thirty-two marks of a great man—the distinguishing physical characteristics of a Buddha. Eventually this knowledge was incorporated into the Vedas as the "Mastery of Reading Physical Characteristics," and all Brahmins were well-versed in this art.

King Suddhodana looked at him with great astonishment and said: "No, no, he will either become a Buddha or an Emperor—that is what everyone else said ... young Brahmin, you must be mistaken."

"I heard what everyone else said my Lord, but this Prince will leave the royal life and become a Buddha. I say this with utmost certainty."

Waves of whispers stirred from every corner of the hall. Royalties from neighboring countries and other noblemen and women looked at the King and the young Brahmin in utter disbelief. A visiting noblewoman from a neighboring state and her lady-in-waiting sauntered towards Queen Mahāmāya to console her.

The King raised his voice with his gaze fixed on the Brahmin Koṇḍañña.

"Do you see any reason for him to leave the palace?"

"Yes, my Lord, if he sees the suffering in this life, if he encounters death, he will leave."

"Leave and do what?" exclaimed the King.

The voices in the hall trailed away and the music stopped. No one dared to break the silence.

Koṇḍañña took a few minutes to have another look at the delicate, white hair on the forehead, in between the eyebrows of the baby prince. The white hair spiraled clockwise to the right. Koṇḍañña's confidence in the significance of this feature grew. Thus with conviction he said, "He will achieve liberation."

A trace of anger was in the King's eyes, but he looked at the gathering with a forced smile: "Liberation … liberation for whom? He has every happiness here in this palace … look at this place … who would ever want to leave this?" Everyone nodded in agreement, and a murmur started as everyone looked around the hall. It was a magnificent palace. The high ceiling of the chamber with its grand sandalwood windows and doors, adorned with beautiful carvings, suggested an abundance of wealth. The throne made of gold and silver, decorated with different shades of blue sapphire gems, made comfortable with cotton cushions, spoke of the luxury and comfort of the palace. The breeze which carried the freshness of the Himalayan Mountains kept the castle built in the foothills, fresh throughout the year. It was a known fact that King Suddhodana, though he was a warrior king, was exceedingly kind and considerate towards his servants compared to other Kings of the nation. Therefore, there was no shortage of young servants, dancers and musicians in the palace. The luxurious rooms and ambiance kept its occupants in such comfort that they were unlikely to leave.

"Liberation for humankind, my King," the Brahmin Koṇḍañña answered before silence fell over the hall once again.

"He could "liberate" everyone while being the Emperor, and he shall be a great Emperor and as he is my son, I say he will stay in my palace and glorify the name of the Sākyans."

Seeing the tension between the King and Koṇḍañña, an elderly Brahmin stepped forward: "He would only do good for the world … to that, we all agree."

"Yes, we agree," all of the hundred and seven Brahmins assented simultaneously. Koṇḍañña stepped back while nodding his head in agreement. King Suddhodana stared at Koṇḍañña, then looked at the elderly Brahmin with a sigh.

"So my king, the most suitable name for your son is Siddhārtha, doer of good."

"Siddhārtha!" the whole gathering resounded in unison.

The king looked pleased, yet troubled.

"Siddhārtha it is," said the King, picking up his newborn son with much love and tenderness. The Queen joined him and took the beautiful Prince Siddhārtha in her hands.

"I cannot believe this young Koṇḍañña! Why would he say something like that?" said an elderly Brahmin to another.

"If Koṇḍañña were uncertain, he would not have declared definitively the boy's destiny, after all, he is one of the wisest Brahmins," said the other.

"One of the wisest, but not the only one," said the elderly Brahmin angrily. "Yet, we cannot ignore his opinion," and he made his way to the King, who was absorbed in thought. Together they both withdrew to a quiet corner and sat with heavy hearts. The elderly Brahmin who also acted as counselor comforted the disturbed King. After a while King Suddhodana, looking much relieved, joined the ceremony and sat next to the Queen Mahāmāya who was cuddling Prince Siddhārtha tenderly in her arms.

"Koṇḍañña, is it true? Will he leave the palace … all this luxury?" a young Brahmin asked Koṇḍañña as he was leaving the palace.

"Yes, he will. I must be alert and ready," replied Koṇḍañña while trying unsuccessfully to hide his overwhelming joy. He made his way out of the palace through the vast throng that had gathered in the garden to see the newborn prince. Koṇḍañña's happiness was far more significant than the collective joy of the crowd.

2

The Renunciation

29 years later …

"Koṇḍañña! It has happened! He has done it! Prince Siddhārtha left the palace last night!" shouted the young Brahmin Vappa as he came running to the hermitage.

Vappa's voice startled Brahmin Koṇḍañña from his sleep. It took him a while to process what he had heard. Then, he darted from his chamber towards Brahmin Vappa.

"Prince Siddhārtha left the palace last night," repeated Vappa. Wise Brahmin Koṇḍañña's heart jolted with joy, his face beamed, and he sat without a word for a while. Four of his Brahmin students sat next to him anxiously.

"I must follow him," said Koṇḍañña. "Where did the Prince go? To which city?" he asked Brahmin Vappa.

"No one knows yet. The Prince's charioteer Channa and his horse Kanthaka are not in the palace. We will know more by the evening. I'll go back to the palace and await more information," said Vappa as he headed towards the palace with Brahmin Bhaddiya.

By late evening the Brahmins Vappa and Bhaddiya came back with more news about Prince Siddhārtha. "The King's soldiers have found Channa while he was returning to the palace, near the city of Ayodhya, and have escorted him back to the palace. He had said that the prince crossed the river Anomā and headed south."

"He has already passed three counties!" said the Brahmin Koṇḍañña, adding, "I am leaving tomorrow morning, anyone who wishes to join, may do so."

"We all would like to come with you," replied the four Brahmins.

It was a long night for Koṇḍañña. He longed to hear this news for quite some time. He remembered the first time he saw Prince Siddhārtha at the naming ceremony. Koṇḍañña was in his early 40's then, and after 29 years he can still remember how he felt when he saw the newborn baby. He recalled his meetings with young Prince Siddhārtha, which were few and under supervision, by the orders of the King. He remembered how intelligent and kind the young Prince was.

Koṇḍañña as a child had learned that one day a Buddha would arise in the world. Inspired by those childhood stories he became interested in a life devoted to spiritual development. Hailing from an affluent Brahmin family, after completing his education, Koṇḍañña chose a spiritual life over matrimony. Koṇḍañña learned that a Buddha would find the solution that liberates humankind from all the sufferings of life. However, at that time no one knew how to fully explain suffering. The news of a future Buddha precipitated a spiritual awakening throughout the country. Many defined suffering in different ways and taught various methods to gain freedom from it, declaring themselves enlightened and preaching different doctrines.

Koṇḍañña also learned from teachers and wise ascetics how to recognize a newborn who has the potential to be a future Buddha. He learned that a Buddha would possess thirty-two distinct physical characteristics at birth. However, there was also a belief that a baby born with these features could either be a Buddha or an Emperor. Thus, young Koṇḍañña spent hours studying, meditating and contemplating on how to distinguish a Buddha from an Emperor. Without arriving at a definitive answer, Koṇḍañña resorted to trusting his inner voice. He thought if he finds a baby with these features, some feature will stand out from the rest and he will know. Koṇḍañña also contemplated that it was an era of spiritual awakening. Thus, it was more suitable for a spiritual leader than a monarch.

Ever since he found Prince Siddhārtha, Koṇḍañña had been studying different doctrines that Brahmins and ascetics practiced. Among all the beliefs, the practice of extreme asceticism fascinated him and he went in search of those who undertook it. However, he did not find anyone who trained in all aspects of asceticism. Every Brahmin or ascetic who practiced it selected only one method of asceticism and continued it throughout his life, which Koṇḍañña thought was unsatisfactory. He was of the opinion that it would take a great man to endeavor in all the aspects of asceticism, and he was confident that such an attempt would bring ultimate liberation. Hence, he learned about extreme austerity in detail. In time, four young students came to study under him: Vappa, Bhaddiya, Mahānāma and Assaji. The Brahmin Koṇḍañña, in keeping with his tradition, taught the Vedas, Tantra and different meditation practices to his Brahmin students, but did not discuss the extreme austerity practices with them.

Koṇḍañña felt overwhelmed by emotions of both happiness and sadness. He wanted to run and find Siddhārtha, but the strength of his limbs did not match the strength of his mind. Koṇḍañña was sure that Siddhārtha would find the ultimate liberation and longed to hear and learn the path to liberation that Siddhārtha would teach. Siddhārtha would become a Buddha. "What exactly does it mean to be a Buddha?" Koṇḍañña pondered.

Early next morning, the five of them left the hermitage in the name of the future Buddha and headed south. They thought that if they went to the Kingdom of Magadha, which is to the south of river Anomā, they might be able to ascertain Prince Siddhārtha's whereabouts. However, when they reached the city, all they heard about was the magnificence of the new ascetic who had just left the town.

"I thought he was a god when I first saw him, his serenity, his beauty … it's beyond words," a man said.

"That's how I felt too. Maybe he is a god, or a Brahma from the heavenly worlds," another man joined.

"No, he is from a royal family. Didn't you hear what our King's soldiers said? He has given up a whole Kingdom in the north," said another.

"And he was destined to be a Monarch, I heard, but has given it all up. How can one do that?" a woman asked in disbelief.

"Oh! I am so happy that I offered him food! He looked so very kind. My heart became peaceful just by looking at his face!" a woman cried with joy.

"I followed after him ... I couldn't go home, I just wanted to follow him ... I followed him to the foot of mountain Pāndawa, then the King arrived, so I left," lamented a young man, feeling sorry for leaving the ascetic's presence.

People marveled at how the new ascetic rejected the offer from King Bimbisāra: "The King has offered him half of the kingdom," exclaimed one man, adding "but he has rejected it."

"Well, of course he would decline, he has already left an entire Kingdom. He is looking for some kind of liberation I heard," stated another young man full of respect towards this new person he saw.

The new ascetic was the talk of the town. Koṇḍañña learned that Prince Siddhārtha had removed his royal clothes and donned a yellow robe. He had become a ascetic. The Brahmins went towards the mountain range hoping to meet Siddhārtha at the foot of Mountain Pāndawa. Unfortunately, ascetic Siddhārtha was nowhere to be seen. The Brahmins too removed their Brahmin attire, accepted robes and begging bowls, and became ascetics in the name of Siddhārtha—the Buddha-to-be.

3

With Guru Ālāra Kālāma

Ascetic Koṇḍañña's urge to see Siddhārtha became much more intense after listening to the people of Magadha. A few months passed without a word on Siddhārtha's whereabouts. Then one day, they heard that a new, divine-looking young ascetic had come to the hermitage of the Guru Ālāra Kālāma. Instantly, Koṇḍañña knew it was Siddhārtha. Next morning the ascetics headed towards the north, crossing the river Ganges, and arriving at where the Guru Ālāra Kālāma was dwelling. But alas! By the time they had reached the hermitage, the ascetic Siddhārtha had just left, having mastered the teachings of Guru Ālāra Kālāma.

Ascetic Koṇḍañña could not believe his misfortune, he sighed mournfully: "I will go to Guru Ālāra Kālāma and ask where Siddhārtha went."

"My friends, you look tired, please come and refresh yourselves, our Guru will meet you soon," the kind words of disciples of Guru Kālāma made Koṇḍañña feel welcomed. A few hours later, after arising from meditation, Guru Kālāma came to see the visitors.

"My friends, did you come looking for Siddhārtha?" asked Guru Kālāma in a very kind and soft voice. "Yes, we have been looking for him for a long time, ever since he left the palace," Koṇḍañña's voice sank. Seeing his sadness, Guru Kālāma encouraged him: "Do not stop looking for him, he is worthy of seeking after for many miles, many days, and even for many years." Hearing this Koṇḍañña felt a sudden warmth of happiness embracing his body, and he asked, "How is he, Guru Kālāma?"

"I have never met anyone as perfect as Siddhārtha in my entire life, and I am sure I never will. His wisdom is like a ... a ... diamond, it pierces through with clarity to the nature of life. His ability to achieve higher levels of concentration is unbelievable. He quickly learned the doctrine; just by mere lip-reciting, he could grasp and master the words of knowledge, the words of my elders. For a moment I thought he was content here, after attaining the ākiñcaññāyatana level of concentration of mind, the base of nothingness."

"What did he say?" asked the ascetic Koṇḍañña eagerly.

"He questioned the result of this practice. He said this teaching does not lead to disenchantment, to dispassion, to cessation. Also, he said it does not lead to direct knowledge, to awakening or freedom from suffering, but only to rebirth in the dimension of Nothingness, arguing that if there is any form of birth, then there shall be aging and death."

"To quote his own words, 'Birth in any realm, in any form, would always lead to death. Which means it does not constitute lasting happiness or freedom from suffering.'"

"Which is something that never occurred to me," mused Kālāma.

Guru Kālāma thought for a while and remarked, "He says this practice is a mental skill and anything that is mind-made is subject to decay; he is looking for ultimate bliss, ultimate freedom from birth and death. My friends, his knowledge surpasses mine; I cannot comprehend what he is looking for."

"He is looking for Buddhahood Guru Kālāma," said Vappa, trying to console him.

"I absolutely admire him, he is a person full of merits, and it would be great if he attains what he is looking for! I have never met such a lovely person," Guru Kālāma sounded sad. Silence took over the conversation. "Please stay here for a while my friends," Guru Kālāma broke the silence by trying to be cheerful. "You have known Siddhārtha from birth. Maybe we can share more about him." But Koṇḍañña, who thought he understood Siddhārtha's rationale for leaving Guru Kālāma, was preoccupied with finding him.

"Oh! Guru Kālāma, we cannot, we desire to find Siddhārtha, but thank you ever so much. We will leave now." The ascetic Koṇḍañña and the group paid respect to the Guru and went towards the village hoping to hear something as to where Siddhārtha had headed.

4

At the Hermitage of Guru Uddakka Rāmaputta

Again, seasons passed without a word about ascetic Siddhārtha. Koṇḍañña became anxious. Every day the five ascetics went in five different directions for their alms and looked for Siddhārtha. They went from village to village, from one hermitage to another. Some days they heard that a young ascetic matching Siddhārtha's description had come to a certain hermitage, and they hurried there only to find out that it was not Siddhārtha but someone else.

One day, ascetic Mahānāma met a student named Gopi of the much respected Guru Uddaka Rāmaputta, whom many treated as if he were a god. Gopi had traveled to a nearby village to buy some medicine two days ago.

This zealous young student Gopi talked about a new hermit that had come to his teacher to learn his teaching: "He is simply awesome! He came here … hmm … three months ago, but now he teaches us," said Gopi as he and ascetic Mahānāma sat for a little rest. "He learnt in two hours a tantra which took me five years to learn, I don't know how he can do that." Mahānāma stopped eating and stared at Gopi. "He sits in meditation for hours, or days maybe … he has answers for all our questions; all of us wait until he comes to the hall to listen to him. He has these bright blue eyes that tell us that we can trust him, and he is so kind, the kindest person I have ever met." Gopi noticed that Mahānāma was listening to him with his mouth slack and said, "I am talking too much, aren't I?"

"Oh no, please tell me, do you know his name?" asked Mahānāma coming back to his senses.

"Oh! Didn't I tell you? It's Siddhārtha," said Gopi.

Mahānāma jumped up with joy: "Thank you Gopi! Thank you! Now I must go, excuse me," and ran to meet the others.

"We will go now. If we hurry, we can reach that hermitage by evening the day-after-tomorrow. I do not want to miss Siddhārtha again," Koṇḍañña hurried. They reached the beautiful monastery near the river Mahi by early evening. As they entered, they noticed Guru Uddaka seated alone under a tree. They greeted him and introduced themselves. Guru Uddaka was happy to meet someone else who knew ascetic Siddhārtha, but the troubled look on his face made Koṇḍañña very uneasy.

"Can we meet ascetic Siddhārtha?" asked Koṇḍañña with respect.

"If only he were here," said Guru Uddaka gently.

Ascetic Koṇḍañña felt as if his stomach had jolted up

and got stuck in his throat. He could not speak, and tears fell from his eyes. "Why didn't you make him stay?" asked ascetic Bhaddiya feeling genuinely sorry for Koṇḍañña.

"Can I stop this river Mahi from falling into the sea?" replied Guru Uddaka.

"What happened? Why did he leave?" asked ascetic Mahānāma puzzled.

"Before coming here, he had been to Guru Ālāra Kālāma," said Guru Uddaka. "Having mastered his teachings, it had occurred to him that the Dhamma taught by Kālāma does not lead to true knowledge and freedom from suffering. And a few months after leaving Kālāma, he realized that the mind could be developed further. To that end, he searched for a teacher who could provide appropriate guidance; it was then that he came in search of me."

They all listened to Guru Uddaka with bated breath.

"He mastered my teachings immediately. There was nothing more I could teach him. He did not find what he was looking for through the highest level of concentration known to me," continued Guru Uddaka.

"With all due respect, is there any other teacher who teaches a greater concentration level?" asked ascetic Bhaddiya naively.

"Not to my knowledge, no," smiled Guru Uddaka, and continued, "His quest is to find how to end birth, and he realised the cessation of suffering cannot be achieved through the level of concentration I teach, the attainment of the base of neither-perception-nor-non-perception. He is looking for a permanent solution, not a temporary one."

"Did he tell you how he is going to find it, or where he is going?" asked Koṇḍañña, his voice trembling.

Guru Uddaka noticed Koṇḍañña's pain and said, "I am afraid he said nothing. But I am sure you will find him, please stay with me for a few days and get some rest."

The ascetic Koṇḍañña could not refuse the great Guru's entreaty. So he agreed to stay and rest his aching feet and heart for a while. Though Koṇḍañña made no mention of it, he approved of Siddhārtha's decision to leave Guru Uddaka since Koṇḍañña firmly believed that practicing austerity was the only way to free oneself from suffering.

5

The Practice of Extreme Austerity

Seasons changed, months passed by without any word about ascetic Siddhārtha. The five ascetics continued their quest of finding Siddhārtha with renewed hopes each morning. On their journey, they came to a village called Senāni in the province of Uruvela. It was a beautiful area with a forest full of lush greenery nourished by the river Nerañjanā (now known as river Niranjanā) which flows from the mountains to the valley where a small community of farmers and shepherds lived. Koṇḍañña suggested that they spend the night in the hut built for wandering ascetics at the edge of the village. Next morning, when the five ascetics were about to leave, another ascetic came from the forest and seeing that they had already occupied the hut, sat under a tree.

Koṇḍañña looked at him from a distance and started walking towards him. The new ascetic looked tired yet determined, cheerless yet courageous, thin yet very handsome, weak yet steady. He sat in a meditative posture with such ease, his skin glowed under the morning sun, and he looked at

Koṇḍañña with his big, beautiful, blue eyes.

"Prince Siddhārtha!" Koṇḍañña shouted with joy.

Siddhārtha recognized Koṇḍañña at once: "Brahmin Koṇḍañña, what a pleasant meeting! But how? What are you doing here? And why are you dressed as an ascetic?"

"My Prince, we became ascetics and left our homes when we heard that you had left the palace, and we have been looking for you ever since," replied Koṇḍañña with tears rolling down, reaching for Siddhārtha with trembling hands. Siddhārtha took Koṇḍañña's hands in both of his own and entered the hut where the other four were waiting impatiently, transfixed by what had happened. After he had introduced the others to Siddhārtha, Koṇḍañña narrated their journey.

Siddhārtha listened patiently and responded, "Yes Koṇḍañña, I left Guru Kālāma and Guru Uddaka Rāmaputta because their teachings do not lead to lasting happiness that I seek, happiness that transcends aging and death and the whole mass of suffering."

"What do you do now my Prince? What have you been doing since then?" asked Koṇḍañña impatiently.

Siddhārtha smiled and said, "I have started practicing extreme asceticism."

"Yes, yes my Prince, I too believe that asceticism is the way to liberation," said Koṇḍañña with great joy.

"Please call me Siddhārtha, or friend, we are all ascetics

now, all at the same level of understanding," said Siddhārtha. "I hope this is the way. In the palace I had all the comforts one could dream of, yet that did not free me from aging and death. Now, this practice of asceticism involves denying comforts and making the body suffer to the extreme. Perhaps this is the way to liberation."

"What practices have you tried so far my Lord, I mean my Pri … I mean my … my friend?" asked Vappa, earnest in his desire to learn about asceticism practiced during that time.

"Well, the Brahmins and wanderers who believe purification comes from food. And they undertake various practices about food. Thinking I should do the same, I began accepting seven morsels per day, from seven houses, and continued this for a month. Then, since it had no impact in purifying my mind, I reduced it to six morsels from six houses. I practiced that for about a month. After that, I gradually reduced my intake of food, and now I accept three morsels from three houses per day."

"Is that a practice?" asked Mahānāma.

"Yes, some ascetics live on seven morsels from seven houses a day for their entire life. Some on six, some on five, and so on, up to one morsel of food from a single house per day. The belief is, since food is a comfort and gives rise to desire, by reducing food one is rejecting comforts and at the same time subduing desire. And it …"

"So you just accept food during your alms-round and reduce the amount you take?" interposed Mahānāma.

"No Mahānāma, there is so much more to it than that," snapped Koṇḍañña, "you cannot accept food from a pot or a bowl, or food offered across a threshold, across a stick, I mean food offered using a stick, or a pestle…"

The ascetic Siddhārtha smiled when he saw the perplexed faces of the young ascetics. His beautiful white teeth shone in the sunlight. Seeing him smile, everyone beamed and relaxed. Siddhārtha's calm demeanor was contagious.

After a minute Koṇḍañña continued: "And you don't accept food from a place where there are two people already eating, nor from a pregnant or a nursing woman, nor from where food is advertised for distribution … hmm."

"Nor from places where dogs lie, or where there are lots of flies," joined in ascetic Siddhārtha.

"What if you do not find suitable offerings? What would you do? Can you accept two morsels of food from one house?" asked Assaji.

"No, I have to be scrupulous in my practice. Thereby I may achieve my goal; I cannot be heedless. So, some days I walk miles to find just one morsel of food," said Siddhārtha while stretching his legs.

"Would you accept any type of food or are there restrictions on that too? Mahānāma asked, feeling sorry for Siddhārtha.

"According to the practice, you do not eat fish nor meat nor consume any fermented drinks, so many tasty foods are unacceptable. I had my share of tasty food while living in the palace," answered Siddhārtha in a humorous tone putting everyone at ease.

"Let us assist you Siddhārtha in your quest. Let us help you while you continue this practice, until you achieve what you are looking for," requested Koṇḍañña.

"What about your meditation and other practices? You will not be able to do that if you start attending to me, won't you?" asked Siddhārtha.

"We can take turns in attending you, and we can learn about asceticism too; we know very little about it," said Assaji, and the others agreed. Thus the five ascetics decided to assist the ascetic Siddhārtha in continuing this practice and becoming a Buddha. They cleared an area nearby the outskirts of the forest, near the River Nerañjanā, and built huts with the help of some villagers. They started learning about the practice in the belief that it was the path to liberation, according to Koṇḍañña's thoughts, and also because no one knew of any other way.

Siddhārtha had visited many ascetics who practiced self-mortification and learned about all the different methods that were available at the time. Many ascetics talked about the practices, yet only a few committed themselves to the practice, deterred by the knowledge that some had died from the rigorous self-mortification techniques. Clearly, it was not a practice for the fainthearted.

During the next three months, the ascetic Siddhārtha reduced the amount of food he accepted on his alms-round to one morsel of food per day. The young ascetics tried to follow

Siddhārtha but gave up after some time.

Each subsequent month, the ascetic Siddhārtha's practice became more intense. He started eating once a day for about a month, then reduced it to once in two days, then once in three days, once in four days, once in five days, once in six days, once in seven days, and finally, he ate only once in a fortnight. He pursued the practice of taking food at stated intervals. Everyone became concerned for Siddhārtha's health, but he did not slacken his effort until, having taken each practice to its extreme, he realized each method did not help him achieve the wisdom and liberation he so earnestly sought.

During this time, when the ascetic Siddhārtha's robe tore, he used shrouds and rags to make a new robe, instead of accepting new robes given by laypeople. Vappa and Bhaddiya cleaned those rags for Siddhārtha using herbs from trees. Following this practice, Siddhārtha gave up fine linen as a way to abolish desire. He also adopted the practice of pulling out hair and beard using sesame seeds. That was a torturous practice carried out by only a handful of ascetics. The idea behind it was unclear, but Siddhārtha wanted to try everything that other ascetics practiced.

"Your delicate skin will not stand this painful practice, my friend," said Assaji while helping Siddhārtha one day, "Your skin is bruised and bleeding!"

Koṇḍañña sat silently beside them. It tore him apart to watch Siddhārtha suffer. With each passing day, his love and admiration for Siddhārtha grew steadily, so much so that he wanted to fall at Siddhārtha's feet and ask him to put an end to this ordeal. But he could not because he was confident that Siddhārtha was the one who would become a Buddha, and he was equally convinced that self-mortification was the way to achieve that lofty goal, no matter how unforgiving it proved to be.

For another few months, Siddhārtha adopted the practice of rejecting seats and spending the day and night in standing and squatting postures. Even to the most daring of people, watching his penances was difficult. The others, except Koṇḍañña, tried to spend as many hours as possible in the standing posture but squatting no one could do for more than half an hour.

"This practice hinders my concentration," Siddhārtha shared his thoughts with Koṇḍañña.

"Your legs are swollen my friend, maybe you should sit down at least for a moment. Even the ascetics who practice this for their entire life, sit and sleep during the night," urged Koṇḍañña.

"I wouldn't sit down because my legs hurt Koṇḍañña, only if this practice proves to be fruitless, I will sit down," replied Siddhārtha continuing his practice.

"Koṇḍañña, come quick, our friend is very sick!" shouted Bhaddiya, having seen Siddhārtha collapsed in the nearby forest. The others hurried towards Bhaddiya, and to their horror encountered ascetic Siddhārtha splayed on the ground, too weak to stand. No one could hold back tears as they carried Siddhārtha to the shade of a tree and helped him regain his strength. The harsh austerities had swelled his legs so much that even mosquito bites drew blood. The strict practice of rejecting seats ultimately did nothing more than make him sick and unable to move for a week.

Having heard about reports of his intense asceticism, people gathered near the ascetic Siddhārtha, seeking an audience and to worship him. However, as the crowd around him grew, Siddhārtha, seeking seclusion, retreated deeper into the dense forest. In such a manner, every six months Siddhārtha and the five ascetics changed their dwelling. They made temporary huts using whatever they could find in the woods. However, Siddhārtha did not want the others to accompany him into the thick forest because that would make it difficult for them to go on alms-round. Hence, living alone in the forest he trained in the discipline known as the practice of extreme seclusion and was not seen for months at a time. By this time Siddhārtha had given up going on alms-round and ate whatever he could find in the forest, and he looked a shadow of his former self.

One day, while practicing extreme seclusion, Siddhārtha asked the five ascetics to help him make a mattress of spikes, which was another way of torturing the body to eradicate desire. Upon completion of their task, the five ascetics looked aghast at the bed of nails they had made for Siddhārtha to lie on.

Everyone could see the bruises on Siddhārtha's body from that day onward. His gold-colored skin which shone under the sun, now blotched with red marks, had lost its glow.

He was utterly indifferent to his body. Dust and dirt which accumulated over his body caked and flaked just as it accumulates over the years at the bole of a tree. He did not even care to rub the dirt off with his hands.

"He should stop this, or else he will die," cried Vappa.

"No one, in the history of austere practice has done as much, we should ask him to stop this Koṇḍañña," joined Mahānāma.

"This is what it takes to become a Buddha. He cannot stop now. I know he shall succeed!" said Koṇḍañña with much faith in Siddhārtha.

On account of Koṇḍañña's wisdom and intelligence and their respect for him, not wanting to challenge nor suggest opposing views, they collectively supported the practice of tormenting and mortifying the body as the way to become enlightened. Yet privately, they hoped no harm would come to their beloved friend on that account. They all asked the gods of the forest to protect this noble person who refused to give up and was willing to go to extreme ends to accomplish the elusive goal of purification and final freedom from all forms of suffering.

6

Such was Siddhārtha's Asceticism

It had been more than three years since the five ascetics met Siddhārtha. And day by day Siddhārtha's practice of asceticism was reaching its maximum intensity. He began the exercise of bathing three times a day, during winter, and laid in scorching sun during the dry season. But thus far he did not gain any knowledge or attain any vision worthy of noble ones.

Siddhārtha entered the small thatched hut that the five ascetics had built for him, Koṇḍañña following behind. After they took their seats, Bhaddiya offered them some juice knowing well that this was the only time that Siddhārtha would accept it, owing to the unbearable heat.

"I am going back to that grove Koṇḍañña," said Siddhārtha.

"Which one? where you spent your winter days, the one near the charnel ground?" asked Koṇḍañña while the others gasped.

"Yes, now we have come to the middle of the hot season,

I can use the heat to scorch the body during the day and spend the nights inside the grove and see if that would help," replied Siddhārtha.

"I wouldn't go there Siddhārtha," interposed Mahānāma "last time I came to see you, you scared me! Those winter nights without even a fire!"

Next morning when the five ascetics woke up, Siddhārtha was not in his hut.

The hot season passed followed by the rains. During the heavy thunder and lightning Koṇḍañña became concerned for Siddhārtha's well-being, so they decided to go into the forest once again to look for him.

After about two days walk into the dense forest, they found Siddhārtha. He was wearing a robe made from tree bark. In fear of the wild animals, the five ascetics cleared a place in the forest and built two huts, one for them and one for Siddhārtha. A task made easier as the ascetics hut building skills steadily improved as they moved from one location to another.

The ascetic Siddhārtha continued his meditation. Koṇḍañña told the others, "Our friend is practicing the trance of non-breathing." They could see, from afar, that Siddhārtha was in severe pain. One thing they had learned about Siddhārtha was no matter how much physical pain he suffered, the pain never invaded the tranquility of his mind.

One morning Siddhārtha said, "I have been trying to attain purification through food according to the ascetics of this austere practice. Yet thus far, I have gained nothing. Therefore, I must intensify this practice—I've decided to live on Indian plums from now on until I realize what I'm looking for."

"Oh good! I know how to make Indian plum juice; you crush the plums and mix with some water to…"

"No Mahānāma," interrupted Siddhārtha with a smile, "only one Indian plum a day will do."

"What!!!" exclaimed Mahānāma in complete disbelief. "How can anyone live on one Indian plum a day!?" protested Mahānāma forgetting what he learned about self-mortification, "And especially you Siddhārtha, look at you! You are just skin and bones."

"I have to try Mahānāma, if I were to die in my efforts to find freedom from suffering, so be it. I will gladly embrace death rather than to live a life beset with imperfections," said Siddhārtha, and no one could find words to reply.

For the next couple of months, Siddhārtha ate only a single Indian plum fruit a day. Then later having made no greater realization, he reduced his intake to a single bean a day. The five ascetics watched as Siddhārtha's body shrank beyond recognition. His backside became like a camel's hoof, and his spine stood forth like corded beads from lack of nourishment; his ribs jutted out, his hair fell out and his scalp shriveled and withered as a raw bitter gourd shrivels and shrinks in the wind and sun.

"Koṇḍañña, he will die, then we will have nothing," said

Bhaddiya, and Assaji soon agreed. "Yes, many months have passed, I have never seen or heard of anyone taking asceticism this far."

"But he is the only one who can find the way to liberation for all; I saw it at the naming ceremony; I am certain that Siddhārtha will find it through this practice. There is no other way, no one knows any other way, this is the only path." Koṇḍañña's stern belief in this practice silenced those who knew less.

After a few more months Siddhārtha reduced his food intake to a single grain of rice, which made him frighteningly weak. He lay in fields for hours not being able to stand up. His beautiful blue eyes sank into the skull and lost their gleam. When he touched his belly skin he could feel his backbone, and when he touched his backbone he could feel his belly skin. He could barely stand up, and he couldn't sit in meditation owing to the pain in his limbs and back.

One evening Koṇḍañña, seated next to Siddhārtha, watched in disbelief as body hair came off his skin as he rubbed his hands and legs to ease the persistent pain. By now the ravages of extreme austerity had taken their toll on Siddhārtha's looks and health.

"Koṇḍañña, I have lived withdrawn from sensuality in body and mind for many years now. With painful exertions, I relinquished and stilled my desire, infatuation, urge, and thirst for sensuality. I practiced asceticism, the extreme of asceticism, and practiced coarseness, the extreme of coarseness; I practiced scrupulousness, the extreme of scrupulousness; and practiced seclusion, the extreme of seclusion. I believed a person who endures pain as much as I have would be capable of knowledge, vision and unsurpassed self-awakening. However, I have gained nothing from this. Whatever painful and agonizing feelings ascetics, Brahmins, or contemplatives of the past experienced due to striving, none endured as much pain as I have; whatever painful and agonizing feelings ascetics, Brahmins, or contemplatives of the present experience due to striving, none have endured as much pain as I have. Koṇḍañña, what more is there to be done in this practice?" asked Siddhārtha in his calm, mindful voice.

Koṇḍañña remained silent since he knew no other methods of asceticism. Siddhārtha gave up living on one grain of rice per day and gradually increased the amount of rice he took. The group lived day-by-day carrying out their activities in silence; there was nothing to be said, and the months passed by.

One morning it all changed. "What's happening? Siddhārtha took the begging bowl and headed towards the village. Has he given up the practice? This is indeed a misfortune, Siddhārtha was so close to attaining enlightenment. Why has he given up? Oh, this is a disaster for all beings, Siddhārtha has given up his quest for freedom from suffering. Oh! This was not supposed to happen," grieved Koṇḍañña seeing Siddhārtha leaving the hermitage with his begging bowl.

"What shall we do now?" asked Vappa and all other ascetics awaited Koṇḍañña's reply.

After a long silence, "We will leave Siddhārtha," replied Koṇḍañña in utter disappointment. The other ascetics sat aghast.

"But it was you who predicted that Siddhārtha would become enlightened, and we left home and became ascetics after him, hoping to hear noble teachings from him."

"You were certain about the whole thing dear teacher, what are you saying now?"

"Maybe I was wrong, maybe I missed something," saying thus Koṇḍañña took his begging bowl and his belongings and headed in the direction opposite to the ascetic Siddhārtha. The others followed him without a word; they all saw Koṇḍañña wiping his eyes as he walked away a defeated man.

7

Thus was Born the Mahā Saṅgha

"Do you feel a change in the weather my dear Koṇḍañña?" asked Bhaddiya while bringing a bowl of water to him.

"Yes, I feel it too, look! Flowers have blossomed too, at this hour of the day!?" Vappa said while stroking a flower, "strange indeed!"

"The weather has become very, how do I say it, soothing. Suddenly I feel very comfortable, and everything around looks calm and quiet, more than any other day," continued Bhaddiya looking around the deer park in which they were staying at Vārānasī.

"Yes, and I thought I saw bright lights descending from the sky to this park, as if gods are gathering," joined Mahānāma who was watching the beautiful clear sky and the rising full moon in July.

The ascetic Koṇḍañña did not join in the conversations; withdrawn, he avoided any participation and discussions since leaving Siddhārtha. No one questioned him about what to do next; except for requesting advice, they all continued their practices and helped each other with respect. They dwelled with heavy hearts, but no one dared to express their feelings.

When he left Siddhārtha, Koṇḍañña not only lost his hope to hear the teachings of a Buddha but also his belief that Siddhārtha would be the one to become a Buddha. He remembered what he saw at the naming ceremony of Prince Siddhārtha. Koṇḍañña thought again and again about the unique thirty-two physical characteristics that distinguish a future Buddha, could he have missed something? Could the sages who taught about these physical characteristics have been mistaken?

In his heart, Koṇḍañña knew that Siddhārtha was right and truly believed in him. Though the stark reality of the situation mocked him to reconsider his opinion, he couldn't bring himself to accept that something had gone wrong.

In his mind, he believed the path to liberation was severe asceticism. As to that, Koṇḍañña knew Siddhārtha practiced asceticism to a greater degree than anyone in the past, surely there was nothing further to be done. Then what went wrong?

Koṇḍañña was lost in a battle between his heart and his mind, and the others felt deeply for him. They were convinced that Siddhārtha was responsible for Koṇḍañña's dismal state, but they were afraid to voice their thoughts.

"Mahānāma, someone is coming this way, look," said Vappa arousing Koṇḍañña from his train of thought.

"At this late hour? Who could it be? Must be another ascetic, he looks serene," said Assaji while everyone strained to see the approaching figure.

"Is that ... Siddhārtha?!?" questioned Vappa with complete bewilderment.

Koṇḍañña's heart gave a jolt, whether, for happiness or sadness, he could not discern. He looked on with eyes fixed at the approaching figure—the Lord Buddha Siddhārtha Gautama.

"It's him! Oh, he looks so majestic, so calm." Assaji went towards their guest forgetting his bitterness towards Siddhārtha for a moment.

"Assaji, come back, we need not welcome him, why is he coming to us anyway?" said Vappa.

"We will offer him a seat since he is royalty, that's enough," said Mahānāma, and the others agreed.

But as the Lord Buddha came near, the five ascetics could not adhere to their agreement. One ascetic went up to the Buddha and set out water so he could wash his feet, while another took His bowl and robes, and still another prepared a seat. Then they all sat near the Lord Buddha.

"How are you dear friend Siddhārtha? You look well," asked Assaji. Koṇḍañña was still silent.

"Dear ascetics, I have attained the Unsurpassed Perfect Enlightenment; I have found the path to freedom from all suffering," said the Buddha with great compassion.

Stunned and surprised, the ascetics were speechless. After a moment's silence, Koṇḍañña was the first to recover, but could only respond in a choked voice: "How could you have achieved enlightenment? Friend Siddhārtha, you gave up the path!"

"Do not address me as an equal, I have found the bliss of Nirvāna, I am a Buddha."

"It is not possible Siddhārtha, it is not possible, you gave up the path," said Koṇḍañña unable to suppress his feelings.

"Have I told you before, as I am doing now, that I have attained Enlightenment?" asked the Buddha.

Those words were enough to change Koṇḍañña's mind, he gave in to his heart, and he wholeheartedly believed that Siddhārtha had become a Buddha. All his life he wanted to listen to the blissful Dhamma taught by a Buddha, and now the moment had come, he acceded and replied:

"No, my Lord."

"Then listen carefully, I will teach," said the Lord Buddha as He set the wheel of Dhamma in motion, preaching the Dhammacakkappavattana Sutta. Along with the five ascetics, gods from every realm were there on that full moon night in July listening to the first discourse of the Lord Buddha Siddhārtha Gautama. In this sermon, the Buddha expounded the Four Noble Truths. He explained suffering, the cause for the arising of suffering, the cessation of suffering – Nirvāna – and the path leading to freedom from suffering. When the Lord

Buddha taught the Four Noble Truths, Koṇḍañña understood. He realized the Four Noble Truths. He realized within himself that "whatever is subject to origination is subject to cessation," and thereby gained the taintless, stainless Dhamma-eye and became the first noble disciple.

Thus was born the Mahā Saṅgha.

At that moment the ten-thousand world system shivered and quivered and quaked, while an immeasurable sublime radiance spread throughout the universe, surpassing that of the gods.

Then the Lord Buddha exclaimed: "Indeed you have realized, Koṇḍañña! Indeed you have realized!" In this way, Venerable Koṇḍañña received the name Aññā Koṇḍañña— "Koṇḍañña who realized."

Aññā Koṇḍañña thus became the first Bhikkhu in Gautama Buddha's Dispensation.

8

Attended by the Tuskers

30 Years Later ...

The squirrels in Veluvana Park were enjoying the warm rays of the morning sun. They had plenty of things to be happy about. It was spring, and the trees were full of fruit. The overflowing little springs around the park sprayed water at them inviting them to play. And the bamboo thicket with new leaves ensured that their nests were safe. Apart from these, there was another reason for them to be happy; the Lord Buddha was residing in this park.

Whenever Lord Buddha and the Mahā Saṅgha came to Veluvana Park, the whole atmosphere in the park changed. The environment became soothing, calm, and serene. The crows, eagles, and snakes stopped hunting the squirrels. The people who came to worship Lord Buddha also brought food to the squirrels. But above all, it was the voice of Lord Buddha that made the squirrels happy. Whenever Lord Buddha spoke, the squirrels stood still and listened to the soothing sound of his voice. They spent more time near the monastery than in the trees during this time. That day, they saw an elderly monk they had never seen before slowly approaching the monastery.

His wrinkled skin and white hair spoke of his age while his calm and composed bearing spoke of his greatness. He walked slowly towards Lord Buddha, who was sitting outside the monastery and bowed down near His feet. He caressed the feet of Lord Buddha with great respect and said:

"My Lord I am Aññā Koṇḍañña, my Lord I am your disciple Aññā Koṇḍañña."

Many Arahants and the other monks who were around had never before seen this monk, so they did not know Aññā Koṇḍañña. Those who knew him were thrilled to see him after such a long time. Thereafter, Arahant Vangīsa, having obtained permission from Lord Buddha, spoke in verse praising Arahant Koṇḍañña:

"This Aññā Koṇḍañña Thero is a great Arahant.
He freed himself from suffering with great effort.
He dwells at ease with a concentrated mind.

Arahant Aññā Koṇḍañña Thero
attained final liberation,
which can only be attained
in the Dispensation of the Lord Buddha,
and only by the diligent.

Arahant Aññā Koṇḍañña Thero
has magnificent qualities.

He possesses the excellent wisdom
of recollecting his previous lives,
seeing the past lives of others,
and the wisdom of knowing that he is free
from all defilements.
He can read others' minds.
He is a son of the Lord Buddha."

Arahant Aññā Koṇḍañña sat beside Lord Buddha and informed him of the reason for his visit.

"My Lord, my time in the world has come to an end. It is time for me to pass away into Nirvāna. I came to worship you one last time and request permission to depart."

"My dear son, where have you decided to pass away into Nirvāna?" asked Lord Buddha.

"My Lord, my attendants live near the lake Mandākini. I have decided to pass away by that lake."

"My dear son, monks like you are rare in this order. Therefore, speak the Noble Dhamma to these monks before you head towards that lake."

The great Arahant Aññā Koṇḍañña worshiped Lord Buddha for the last time and rose into the sky. Then, while performing a great miracle, he taught the beautiful and sublime Noble Truths to the monks. Afterward, he traveled through the sky toward the lake Mandākini.

Arahant Aññā Koṇḍañña always enjoyed seclusion. The lake Mandākini at the foot of the Himalaya Mountains provided a perfect home for him. Aññā Koṇḍañña and his fellow students, Vappa, Bhaddiya, Mahānāma, and Assaji, realized the Four Noble Truths and became a fully enlightened after listening to the Anatta Lakkhana Sutta at the Deer Park in Vārānasī. After becoming an Arahant, Aññā Koṇḍañña stayed near Lord Buddha along with the other Arahants and taught the Noble Dhamma to others. Gradually, the disciples of Lord Buddha, the Mahā Saṅgha comprised of great Arahants, grew. After a few years' time, Arahant Aññā Koṇḍañña worshiped Lord Buddha and requested to live a secluded life in the foothills of the Himalayas.

The lake Mandākini, which was near the Gandamāna hill of the Himalayas, spread over nearly five-hundred kilometers and was filled with crystal-clear water. While standing on its banks, the expansive lake extended as far as the eye could see, adorned with colorful water lilies. The remote forest surrounding the lake had many delicious fruits and the weather was always comfortable. Apart from the butterflies, birds and other small animals, the forest was also occupied by a herd of tusker elephants who belonged to the Noble caste called "Chaddanta." Those tuskers descended from a herd that attended Paccekabuddhas who had lived there in the past. For this reason, the lush forest was known as the Chaddanta Forest.

When Arahant Aññā Koṇḍañña went to live by the lake Mandākini the tuskers were jubilant. Keeping up with their ancestral practice they attended Arahant Aññā Koṇḍañña with great respect and love. They cleaned a cave for the great Arahant and cared for him in every way they could. Eight thousand tuskers looked after the great Arahant for twelve years.

Arahant Aññā Koṇḍañña, on having returned from Veluvana Park, bathed for the last time in the lake Mandākini. Having entered his cave and mindfully laid down on his right side in the Lion's Posture, with one foot overlapping the other, he gradually entered refined levels of concentration throughout the night, and by early morning passed away into Nirvāna.

But the chief tusker, unaware of this, came to the cave in the morning, as usual, to attend to the Arahant. Everyday in the morning Arahant Koṇḍañña came out of the cave on time to accept fruits offered by the tuskers. However, on this day he was late. The chief tusker wondered, "Could he be sick?" and gently grunted to make his presence known, but there was no response from within the cave. The tusker then peered into the cave and was relieved to see that the Arahant was asleep. "Oh! The great Arahant is well. He's still sleeping."

The tusker waited for some time, but the Arahant did not rise from his sleep. Impatient and worried, the chief tusker slowly stretched his trunk inside the cave. The tusker extended his trunk beside the Arahant's nostrils and felt for the Arahant's breath. Alas! The great Arahant does not seem to be breathing. Instinctively, the tusker placed the tip of his trunk over the Arahant's heart, feeling for a pulse: "Oh! How can I bear this? The Arahant's heart has stopped beating. The incomparable field of merit, the Great Arahant Aññā Koṇḍañña, who helped us accrue a lot of merit, has passed away."

Unable to bear the pain, the chief tusker trumpeted and

summoned the other tuskers, announcing: "My dear friends, our great field of merit, our beloved Arahant Koṇḍañña, has passed away. He has left us once and for all." Hearing the eulogy of their chief, all 8,000 tuskers trumpeted in unison and the resonance from their trumpeting shook the entire Mandākini valley.

Their poignant trumpeting was heard by the gods and brahmas in the heavenly worlds. The gods and brahmas placed the sacred body of great Arahant Aññā Koṇḍañña on a pyre in homage. Eight thousand tuskers came to pay their last respects to the Arahant, circumambulating the funeral pyre three times. Then the gods set the pyre alight. After the fire had been extinguished, and the body cremated, there remained the relics of Arahant Aññā Koṇḍañña. A stūpa was built in honor of the great Arahant enshrining his relics. Henceforth, there remained only the relics for the pious to venerate in the name of the great Arahant Aññā Koṇḍañña.

Homage to the great Arahant Aññā Koṇḍañña—the first monk in the lineage of the Noble Saṅgha in Gotama Buddha's Dispensation!

Epilogue

01. This Dhamma has a wonderful taste. When I heard that excellent Dhamma, I gained great confidence in it. This Dhamma taught by the Supreme Buddha is a passion-free teaching that leads to complete detachment.

02. There are various objects in this world. I think that the thoughts connected with these colorful objects arousing lust, stir up the whole world.

03. Just as dust blown by the wind settles when it rains, so lustful thoughts fade away when one understands them with wisdom.

04. With developed wisdom, when one contemplates all conditioned things as impermanent, he becomes disenchanted with suffering. This is the way to purification.

05. With developed wisdom, when one contemplates all conditioned things as suffering, he becomes disenchanted with suffering. This is the way to purification.

06. With developed wisdom, when one contemplates all phenomena as non-self, he becomes disenchanted

with suffering. This is the way to purification.

07.   This elder Koṇḍañña followed the Buddha very closely. This monk is strong in energy. That is why he could eliminate birth and death. He perfected living the holy life.

08.   There is a huge flood. There are snares everywhere. There are strong spears and there is a mountain hard to split. This elder broke all the spears, destroyed all the snares and split into pieces the mountain that was hard to split. He crossed over the flood and reached the far shore. He is a meditator. He is released from the bond of Māra.

09.   If a monk is conceited, vain, and delights in the association of evil friends, he will sink down into the whirlpool called anger and drown in the great flood of saṁsāra.

10.   The wise monk who is not conceited, not vain, and who acts prudently, restraining sense bases, and associating with noble friends, will put an end to suffering.

11.   His hands and legs are very thin like the knots of the kāla plant. His veins are popping out. He knows very well the purpose of taking food. He has a strong, brave heart.

12.   He goes to the thick forest to meditate. There, when he is attacked by mosquitos and harmful insects, he

endures them with clear mindfulness, like a king elephant in the battlefield.

13. I don't desire death nor do I desire life. Like a person who is awaiting his monthly salary, I am awaiting my time to attain final Nibbāna at passing away.

14. I don't desire death nor do I desire life. With clear mindfulness and awareness, I am awaiting the day to attain final Nibbāna at passing away.

15. The Great Teacher's instruction has been respectfully followed by me. The Buddha's path has been fully followed by me. I lowered the heavy load of defilements. I rooted out the fetters of existence.

16. I became a monk with the wish to achieve one goal. That, I have achieved. So, what do I need anyone else for? (I am liberated from everything.)

(These verses were said by Arahant Aññā Koṇḍañña)

Mahamegha English Publications

Sutta Translations :

Stories of Sakka, Lord of Gods
Stories of Brahmas
Stories of Heavenly Mansions
Stories of Ghosts
The Voice of Enlightened Monks
The Voice of Enlightened Nuns
What Does the Buddha Really Teach?
What Happens After Death? Buddha Answers
This was Said by the Buddha
Pali and English Maha Satipatthana Sutta

Dhamma Books :

Mahamevnawa Pali-English Paritta Chanting Book
The Wise Shall Realize
The Life of the Buddha for Children
Buddhism

To order online, please go to amazon.com